Buying Stocks

How to Build Wealth Fast by Investing in the Stock Market. The Layman's Guide to Buying and Selling Stocks

Contents

Introduction 7

Chapter 1: The Basics 10

Chapter 2: Stock screening process............................. 23

Chapter 3: Buying stocks 34

Chapter 4: Buying stocks online through a broker 67

Chapter 5: Buying stocks without a broker 79

Chapter 6: Buying stocks below market price 84

Chapter 7: When to sell stocks...................................... 88

Chapter 8: Mistakes to avoid and golden nuggets of

advice 100

Conclusion... 110

prohibited and any storage of this document is not allowed unless with written permission from the publisher. All rights reserved.

The information provided herein is stated to be truthful and consistent, in that any liability, in terms of inattention or otherwise, by any usage or abuse of any policies, processes, or directions contained within is the solitary and utter responsibility of the recipient reader. Under no circumstances will any legal responsibility or blame be held against the publisher for any reparation, damages, or monetary loss due to the information herein, either directly or indirectly.

Respective authors own all copyrights not held by the publisher.

The information herein is offered for informational purposes solely, and is universal as so. The presentation of the information is without contract or any type of guarantee assurance.

The trademarks that are used are without any consent, and the publication of the trademark is without permission or backing by the trademark owner. All trademarks and brands within this book are for clarifying purposes only and are the owned by the owners themselves, not affiliated with this document.

Introduction

While there once was a time when stocks were the playthings exclusive to the wealthy, in the last few decades we've seen more and more people with average wallet sizes buying stocks than at any other time in history. No longer a tool reserverd for the rich increase their riches, stocks are now seen as a legitimate means that anybody can use to generate wealth and prepare for eventual retirement. If you are a first time investor, however, it is important for you to educate yourself prior to buying stocks of any kind.

The advantages to buying stocks as an investment strategy are many. Most studies show that the stock market has netted a far greater return on investment over the last seventy years than almost any other type of wealth creating instrument. Though other investment vehicles such as bonds, certificates of deposit, and savings accounts may generate a more consistent - but much smaller - rate of return, stocks are still seen as the vehicle by which even the middle class can raise their economic standing.

The dangers, unfortunately, are equally obvious. Buying stocks can be inherently risky proposition, as you are typically investing in the profitability of an enterprise over which you exercise no control. Nevertheless, there are steps you can take to greatly limit your risk of loss - but that requires constant research and vigilance on your part, as well as the guidance of a respectable brokering agent.

The main reason so many investors feel that they get burned by the markets when they are buying stocks is that they take a short term view of investment strategy. Few people are wise enough - or lucky enough - to make a fortune in the stock market in a short period of time.

The vast majority of those who amass wealth through investing do so over a prolonged and patient period of time.

The surest way to protect yourself from large losses is by developing of a strategy that relies upon steady performance by reputable companies over the long term. Educate yourself about the histories and products produced by the companies that you're interested in, and keep and eye toward the general trends in those industries. With a little care, patience and some learning, pretty much anyone can successfully build wealth by investing in stocks.

Chapter 1: The Basics

So what exactly is a stock? A share of stock represents a fractional ownership stake in a business corporation. Corporations issue stocks in order to raise money for their business operations. Individuals and organizations that buy these stocks become part owners of the business. The more stocks one purchases the greater the fraction of the business one owns.

With the purchase of stock an investor assumes the rights and responsibilities of a part owner in the business no matter how small his stake in the business. One of those rights is the right to elect the board of directors. The board of directors oversees the operations of the company. They are also responsible for selecting the Chief Executive Officer (CEO), who runs the day to day operations of the company and reports to the board. Investors also have a right to receive dividends if dividends are declared. The amount of dividends an investor receives is based on the amount of stocks they own. Companies declare dividends as a way of sharing profits, but they are not obligated to do so.

Why would one invest in the stock of a company? The primary reason that investors invest in stocks is hoping to sell them for a higher price than they bought it for. Hence the popular saying, buy low, sell high. Some investors also invest in stocks in order to earn a steady income from regular dividend payments.

Stocks can be classified according to certain investment characteristics that they posses.

Stocks of high quality corporations that maintain a leadership position in their industry are usually classified as BLUE CHIP stocks examples include Microsoft, Apple, IBM, and Coca-Cola. These stocks are generally considered safe investments and are favored by cautious investors.

Stocks that pay a high portion of their profits as dividends to investors are termed INCOME stocks. They are sought out by investors who want to earn a steady income stream from their investments. Stocks of Public utilities are good examples of income stocks.

Stocks that move as the economy moves are referred to as CYCLICAL stocks. When the economy experiences a downturn they do poorly and when the economy is booming they do great. Examples of such stocks are auto industry stocks, steel stocks and industrial chemical stocks.

Then there's stocks that are immune from the general economic condition, and they are known as DEFENSIVE stocks. These stocks are not seriously influenced by what is going on in the general economy. Good examples of these are grocery, alcohol and utilities stock. The demand for their products and services remains constant in good or bad times.

Stocks that are expected to report higher than average earnings and sales revenues and reinvest most of their profits are often classified as GROWTH stocks. Growth stocks are often highly sought after because their stock price tends to rise quickly. Growth stocks can be found in any sector, but they are usually found in the technology and pharmaceutical sectors. Eventually, a growth stock will stop growing at an above average rate. Examples of past growth stocks include Microsoft, Cisco systems, Genentech, Starbucks and McDonalds.

We also have penny stocks, which are highly speculative stocks in a company with little or no real value other than its uncertain growth potential.

Investors looking to buy or sell stocks simply contact their broker, and then place an order for a specific amount of stocks. The broker then states the bid price-the highest price buyers are willing to pay for a stock-and the ask price-the highest price sellers are willing to sell a stock for. The investor then decides whether to place a market, stop or limit order. A market order instructs the broker to buy or sell at any available price and it's executed immediately. A limit order, on the other hand, is an order to buy a stock at no more, or sell a stock at no less, than a specific price, within a specific time limit.

A stop order much like a limit order is only executed when a price is reached, the difference being that a stop order becomes a market order when that price is hit and the order is executed at whatever available price. So if an investor with a stock worth $90 places a stop order to sell at a price of $80, once the price of the stock drops to $80, the order becomes a market order and then the trade is executed at the best available price. Once the trade is executed, the broker then provides confirmation to the investor. Most trades are usually executed in less than a minute.

The Two Main Types of Stock

In addition to the types of stocks just discussed, the market has two issues of stock to accommodate different types of investors: common stock and preferred stock. As a very general rule, the benefits of common stock tend to be more geared for individual investors while those of preferred stock tend to be more geared to the needs of institutional investors such as pension funds, mutual funds, and banks.

Common Stocks

Aptly named, the common stock is what most people think about when they hear the word stock. It's also the kind of stock most widely bought and sold, or in investor lingo-traded. It represents basic ownership of part of a company, as was described in the beginning of this lesson. The owner of one share of common stock gets one vote, or one proxy, on company matters. As stated earlier, two shares equal two votes and so on.

When discussing types of investments, you will often hear terms such as financial "instruments" and "vehicles." These terms are not "financial terms" which imply anything significant but simply words which are used interchangeably instead of less professional sounding terms such as "things" or "stuff."

If you had bought stocks of an apple company, the value of the company and subsequently its stock would decrease if there was a deep freeze that destroys the apple crop. You would then have suffered what's called a capital loss.

Capital gains and losses are one of the two ways stocks make and lose money (the other being dividends). In addition, however, other factors such as the taxes on capital gains should always be taken into consideration. Current capital gains taxes are so high as to often negate much of a stock's potential earnings and make many stocks unattractive to investors for that reason. As with any investment, you always run the risk of losing the initial money you invested (capital loss). While in such a case it would offer little if any consolation, you would, at least, receive a tax credit for the money you lost.

When the Widget Company makes money by selling all those Widgets, the owners of the stock get a proportional cut of the profits in the form of a dividend. The investor has the choice to take the dividend as a payment after paying taxes on the profit, or reinvesting it to buy more stock. Dividends are related to capital gains in that any company which is consistently making profits and paying them out in dividends will soon be discovered as a great company. For that reason, the value of the company would eventually rise and create a capital gain for its owner when he or she sells the stock.

Preferred Stock

Preferred stock is different from common stock in that preferred stock owners get their dividend payments before the common stock owners. Also, should the company go out of business, preferred stock owners get paid their share of whatever's left before the owners of common stock get paid?

So why isn't everyone buying preferred stock? First, companies don't issue preferred stock until after common stock has been issued, so there's less of it. Second, preferred stock owners don't generally get proxy rights. Third and most important, preferred stock owners usually get paid a preset dividend regardless of how much money the company makes.

Further confusing things, companies can issue any number of different preferred stocks, or classes. Usually, the different kinds are labeled A, B, C, etc., and each class can have a different price or dividend. These classes are highly flexible regarding their similarities and/or differences to each other. This flexibility is necessary to accommodate the circumstances of the issuing company at the time. For that reason, it would be difficult if not impossible to provide a complete listing of preferred stock classes anywhere. As always, the responsibility of discovering the nuances of each class is left up to the investor.

Terminology

There's a few important terms that you should be familiar with before you begin buying and selling stocks. Here's the most essential ones:

-**Ask.** How much it will cost to buy the stock. The price that the seller is willing to take.

-**Bear Market.** A period of time where the stock declines in value. This is often accompanied by pessimism from investors.

-**Bull market.** The opposite of bear market. A period of time where the stock rises in value.

-**Bid.** How much a buyer is willing to pay.

-**Close.** The stock's price when the trading day ends.

-**Dividend.** A payment made regularly by a company out of its profits to its shareholders.

-**Fundamental analysis.** The process of examining the financial wellbeing of a company and its future potential.

-**Liquidity.** The ability to sell or buy a stock without the transaction affecting too much the stock's price. It could also mean how easy it is to buy or sell a share.

-**Margin.** Using borrowed money to trade for more than what you currently have in your account.

-**Market order.** A buy or sell order that is executed immediately at the current market prices.

-**Moving average.** An average of the stock's price over a period of time, used to give an idea of the stock's trend.

-**Price to earnings ratio (PE ratio).** The relation between how much the stock's price and how much the company earns for each share of stock.

-**Quote.** The stock's bid, ask and last price at a certain point during the trading day.

-**Volatility.** A reflection of the degree to which the stock's prices rises and falls over time. A stock is considered highly volatile when its price goes up and down often over a period of time.

-**Yield.** The % of a stock's price that's paid out in a dividend.

Chapter 2: Stock screening process

While it is true that financial ratios are the main ingredients of any stock selection process, be cautioned that there is no single financial ratio or statistic, that when isolated, will provide a greater chance of guaranteeing market outperformance.

When a single measure is used to find stocks to invest, the output is likely to be stocks concentrated in one industry. The goal of any stock selection system should be to combine financial ratios and statistics in a way that mitigates the weaknesses of the individual factors and combines them to form a quality list of potential stock investments.

The number of components in your stock screening process can be infinite when looking for winning stocks. It is possible that some of the criteria may appear in multiple categories, the process of finding the best stocks, applies filters at different layers to focus on stocks that meet your investment criteria.

Universe

The initial criteria are the stock universe which includes the industry, sub industry and the grouping of the stocks to be filtered. Some Investors like to focus on companies in a certain type of business where returns may be more stable or predictable. In certain industries, some financial measures are stressed. Dividend yields may be more important for utilities and real estate than for information technology companies.

Stock data

Stock data includes measurements such as the price, volume, share float, short term interest ratio, and market cap. These indicators are used to determine the value of particular stocks.

Stock performance

The stock performance will illustrate how the stock performed over different periods of time and measures the risk level.

Sales and Profitability

Sales and profitability will determine the actual company performance. Historically, stocks that perform well will have increasing sales revenue.

Liquidity

Liquidity ratios will emphasize the cash position of the company. Stronger ratios may mean less debt, with more cash available to grow the business by making acquisitions or funding capital improvements.

Valuation ratios

The most widely followed ratio is the Price/Earnings ratio. The valuation ratios can be used as an indication as to how the stock price compares to other financial components. All the ratios have the stock price or a component of it as the numerator to indicate whether the stock is valued correctly.

Growth rates

Growth rates can indicate the components that are expected to increase in the future. Growth rates of some financial measurements are helpful in determining whether the company is valued properly. There are also some miscellaneous factors that can be used to find suitable stock for investing. Analyst's coverage, institutional and insider ownership as well as debt ratings can indicate the health and stability of the company.

Before doing any stock investing, remember to have a clear idea of what the money is to be used for in the future as this will help to shape the choice of the investment vehicle. A self evaluation will determine your risk tolerance and when the money will be needed.

Your stock selection process may eventually reduce the need for a broker or financial adviser and allow you to find the best stock based on selected criteria. It can also give the investor a better knowledge of the stocks to invest in and better decisions on whether to buy, hold or sell it.

Finding stocks to invest in is not a complicated process. It helps to have some basic knowledge of investment terms. The most important trait in the selection; process is first to know yourself and what you're looking for when you buy stocks

Other important considerations

Owning the shares of a particular organization at some point of time in life is a dream for most of the people but many decide not to take action due to the inherent risky nature of stocks. However, with a bit of research, you can get great ROIs with minimal risk. Here, are a few tips to buy stocks while minimizing risk.

It is always necessary to collect the certain information about the organization whose stocks you are aiming to buy. The information you should be looking for is the performance of the organization for at least the last eight (8) weeks, but preferrably more than that, up to 52 weeks.. No one can see the future, but this can give you an idea of what the company's performance Look out for the future of the organization and how it is going to perform in short span of time. Research what are the company's main products or services. What advantage does it have over its competitors? Do you think the company will be relevant in the following months and years? The better you understand a company, the easier it will be to make good investment decisions. Along the way, you'll also want to keep up with the company's news. Sometimes, there are large stock movements driven by compelling new announcements or products, or sometimes new management changes. You should also keep an eye out for industry conditions that may affect the entire industry group as a whole either positively or negatively.

It is advised that you do not buy stocks based on the recommendations given by stock brokers or other people. It is quite possible that such advice is created based on rumors and sometimes might lead to scams. The stocks bought with the lots of research and analysis always have the potential of giving back the best returns.

It also seems that every time the stock market enters a downward cycle, there is a chorus of voices raised in condemnation of the system. Most of those who criticize the markets constitute the small investor class or are advocates for that group, and the most common complaint is that the market is too complex or unpredictable for most individuals to understand.

Companies go bankrupt, and small investors often lose their investment, all because they lack the basic knowledge necessary to ensure that their investment is as protected as it can be. One key to this protection is for anyone buying stocks to educate themselves on the different types of stock available.

Remember that there are two primary types of stock available for investors: common stock and preferred stock. They each have their advantages and disadvantages, and each represent a different level of investment and ownership of the company in question. Before you begin buying stocks, it is important for you know the differences of these two types so that you can assess the risk of each and make your investment decision accordingly.

Common stock is the type of stock with which most people are familiar. When you are buying stocks labeled common, you are basically purchasing shares in the company. Due to capital growth, common stocks yield the highest returns over time, but at a greater risk.

That risk is most pronounced in situations where a company goes bankrupt - an event that places common stock owners at the end of the line of those eligible to receive money in the bankruptcy proceedings (after the creditors, bondholders, and preferred stock owners).

For those who would rather use the safe route, and wish a smaller but less risky return on their investment, preferred stocks are the way to go. Those buying preferred stocks are guaranteed a fixed dividend of return, as well as preference over common stock holders in the event that the company is dissolved. Preferred stock, however, can be repurchased by the company at any time, without warning or reason.

Within these two types of stock, companies are free to develop customized options in many forms - including limiting the voting rights of shareholders. These divisions of stock within the same company are generally designated Class A stock, Class B stock, etc. Before buying stocks, you should always research exactly what you are buying, so that you know what your rights and obligations will be.

Chapter 3: Buying stocks

WHY BUY STOCKS?

Contrary to what we may have believed during our childhood years, there's no way to make money grow on trees. However, there are several ways to make money while you sleep, and one of those is by investing in the market. This is one of the many benefits when you buy stocks. You do not have to lift so much as a pointer finger to click the mouse before you see results.

So what else? Sure, it sounds magically to buy stocks and have money shooting out your ears, but let's be honest, that rarely happens. Still, it is not as black and white as that may seem. There are a few other benefits with stock buying that are not necessarily a million bucks that anyone can take advantage of.

Investment is the most common benefit of purchasing stock. Consider the money inflation you have to deal with at an alarming pace. You can hardly enter a restaurant without noticing price increases within a year. Your savings plan, no matter how good it might seem, is just not going to keep up with the alarming inflation rate that we experience in this day and age. Stocks are a great investment that will work with a rising economy, instead of letting your profits linger slowly behind.

Even if you are not a tough risk player in the stock market, you too can still take pleasure in some of the benefits that the stock market has to offer. It is the easiest way to make money, and the investment opportunity is not easy to pass up.

Getting started with the principles of stock market trading is crucial when going ahead with investment plans. But, thorough analysis of stats has to be done before starting in this journey. There are two most important and common ways of buying stocks. The first one is through brokerage and the next one is through DRIPS and DIPS.

If you want to ask a difficult question to an investor, ask him or her how much it will cost when to buy stocks. You will probably get a few puzzled looks and then hear an answer similar to, "That greatly depends on several things." In the stock market, the truth of the matter is that once an initial public offering has ended, there are a number of factors that influence the price of buying stocks and in order to understand stock price factors, you need to understand some of the variables behind them.

Buying stocks using brokerages have proved to be one of the best and easiest ways of purchasing stocks. Brokerages can be classified into two depending on the expense incurred. These are full services brokerages and discount brokerages. Full service brokerages are a wee bit too amicable to the expensive side. The functionalities of this brokerage type are extended for the ease and comfort of the customers. They essentially concentrate their functioning in the management of the accounts of their customers. They assist the customers with legal as well as expert advice, and these all can be counted as the reasons why this scheme is so expensive from a customer standpoint.

The discount brokers function a lot differently. They don't provide any expert advice or legal support. They assist the customers in buying them at a very low commission rate. There was a time when the entry to the stock market trading was confined to the people who were financially sound and strong. Later, the internet boom as well as the explosion of online stock trading marked the entry of discount brokers to this arena, which enabled literally everyone who is interested in giving it a try in trading stocks. The stock broker, who is a discount broker in the context won't come up and advice each and everyone personally, instead they offer generalized tips in stock trade. Hence discount brokerages have proved to be the best economic way for investing and buying them, for an average person.

DRIP is dividend reinvestment plan and DIP is dividend investment plan. Both DRIP and DIP are excellent plans in stock trade for buying them proposed by various reputed organizations or companies. This plan is very straight and simple since the plan let the customers or share holders to buy or purchase the funds of the respective companies directly. Dividend reinvestment plans offer a great opportunity for its share holders to invest their money, irrespective of whether the amount is small or huge. Apart from that, the shareholders are allowed to invest with the flexibility of investing at regular or discrete intervals of time.

Effect of Opening and Closing Prices when buying stocks

Typically, the price will open close to the closing price the previous day. However, stock price breakouts occur when those buying stocks sense an event that could radically change the value of a company and its stock value. Factors that motivate those buying stocks include things that impact production, public perception and overall profitability. As a result, a company will likely see up or down movement in its stock price.

Conversely, the closing price of a stock can have an effect on the next day's price. There tends to be a carry-over effect from close to open that reduces stock volatility. Without any significant Wall Street news overnight, the opening price and the closing price will likely be very similar.

Prices Jump

You will quickly discover when you buy stocks online the prices for the shares will rarely stay the same for long. With the way the global economy works especially with the cost of materials for production and jobless rates that jump sporadically, you will see that the price of a share or stock could be all over the charts. You could make a purchase of stocks at a rate of $3.30 USD a share and two days later you could see the same stocks being offered for $2.65 USD a share.

Knowing when the stocks are going to rise and fall is anyone's guess. If you want to have a better chance at predicting what the share will do in regards to cost, you would be best served to hire a stock broker to manage your account.

The stock broker is paid by you to not only watch the market for any sudden changes, they are also there to bring to your attention any possible trends that they may see developing. This can help you when you are going to buy stocks online, as you will be able to gauge the lowest options for buying in.

A Fresh Start

Each day when the stock market opens, it is a new day. Those buying stocks will help determine the stock prices. A stock that was a strong buy yesterday may be sending off sell signals to savvy investors today. A stock that was struggling today might be tomorrow's hot stock. The key to a stock's value is what people are willing to pay for it. Buying stocks is a perception game. There were people who never thought Google stocks would hold their IPO, let alone rise to over $500 per share. Like in most things in life, beauty or potential is in the eye of the beholder for those buying stocks.

Forget what you've heard. It's not always about greed and fear! While it is true that emotional factors motive prices for the people buying stock, the market will always find the true value of a stock, and give advantages to those who are able to properly read the investment timing. An event in the news may affect the price of buying a stock but the result will only be temporary.

HOW TO BUY STOCKS - THE BASIC NECESSITIES

Learning how to buy stocks and sell them for a profit is not as hard as most people make it out to be. It is, however, not so easy that any regular Joe can make a living off it right then and there without any research or knowledge. Being prepared is key, which is why you need to make sure that you have all of the following before you even think of buying stocks:

Knowledge

Although it may sound obvious, this is the single most important requirement you must have, as well as the most difficult one to obtain. It is for this very reason that it is recommended to continue expanding your stock trading knowledge as much as you can. There are courses available out there that include simulations so that you can practice before using real money. This can make all the difference, especially when you consider the complex machinations that drive the stock market.

Investment goals

Once you have an idea of what stock trading is all about, the next thing that should be settled are your investment. Of course, making money is the main objective here, but such a broad objective will not help you when faced with short-term dilemmas. Without investment goals, you may end up making decisions that you will regret in the long run. These short-term investment goals also help you keep track of your progress and how well you're doing in the long run. Meeting and achieving these goals gives you a sense of accomplishment that will help fuel your desire to learn more about the stock market. For example, are you only interested in safely increasing your income by a conservative 5-10% every year? Then the approach you would take would be very different to the investor that has a more aggressive goal of 30% in mind.

Broker

The broker is your direct link with stock exchange market, and your choice will greatly influence your future as a stock investor. One of the best ways to find a good broker is to simply ask friends, family and colleagues for referrals. If you do not have any such connections, then you can simply browse through a Wall Street magazine and keep an eye out for brokers on the advertisements. Just make sure that you gather as much information about your broker as you can before you start a working relationship with him or her. This will save you a lot of headaches in the long run.

Capital

Of course, you need money to make money, which is why you need a sufficient amount of capital that's in line with your investment goals before you start. In most cases you won't need hundreds of thousands of dollars to get started. More money simply means you can spend more to earn more. You do need at least $25,000 if you want to invest in individual companies, although you can invest $100 in mutual funds - which is related to but different from stock trading.

Other basic requirements

Once you are in the stock trading game, you will then want to find the right tools to help you do transactions and gather information. A reliable internet connection is a must, as you will find a lot of resources to show you how your stocks are doing - charts, graphs, values and much more. You will also be able to quickly message your broker to buy or sell stocks. A phone connection is another essential tool if you want to buy or sell stocks on the go. This is especially important when you learn how to read stock charts from non-Internet sources, like through television or the newspaper.

BASIC DO'S AND DON'TS

The world of high finance revolves around major flows of commodities and money, and it's important to avoid taking as many missteps as possible.

As a prospective day trader or a trader on longer terms of engagement, the first thing you will want to do is to set aside money. This money should be something you can afford to lose - sure, it will hurt to lose it, but losing it will not cripple your life. That is because majority of individual investors stand to make losses in the securities exchange. The stock market is not a gold mine, instead it is a roulette table where fortunes can change in minutes and seconds. Make sure you can survive even after losing the money.

Next is setting up a trading account, which we'll talk more about later. That means looking for a stock brokering firm that will accept your capital. Some discount brokerages will accept as low as USD2500 for a margin account, while others will set the minimum higher. More importantly, you will want to be able to do trading online, so you can cut out the latency involved in calling up your broker for buying and selling. Market regulators are looking to increase the minimum though, so move quickly.

Before engaging in any online transactions, make sure you have a secure connection. At the very least, you should enable your browser's secure transmission capabilities, like SSL. You can do more than just that though. If you are on a wireless network, use encryption and set a password on your network. As much as possible, conduct your online transactions from just one computer. Also, clear your browser's temporary information cache after each use, or use private browsing sessions so you won't forget.

Once you've secured your position, you can start buying. One mistake you will want to avoid is to join a buying rush heedlessly. Sometimes these rushes are caused by hype, and thus they could crash easily. Make sure you know the tricks of how to read and interpret stock charts so you can see if buying is justified or it's just a lemming rush.

It is a simple thing to buy stocks, but buying stocks and gaining a profit from selling them requires a set of basic knowledge. You need to know how to read stock charts and how to analyze trends and predict future price movements. As mentioned, taking a class or a course online that helps you develop your skills and do simulations is highly recommended. Strategy development will be up to you, though if you know a successful trader you might want to ask for advice or if you could sit in on a trading session of his or hers.

FACTORS TO CONSIDER

When we buy stocks, we are investing in companies that we want to own equity in. Investors buy shares through agents, brokers, or through the company they want to buy in. When you decide to buy shares in a company, there's a few important factors that we should keep in mind.

Consider the company you want to own equity in and the environment in the market at that particular period. If the market is going through a recession, you should look into companies that offer products that are necessary in life. A company that offers consumer goods or household items is a suitable choice when the market is going through a recession because they are required in all types of economic situations.

If you decide to buy penny stocks when the market is positive and rising, growth shares are a suitable option to invest in because at this point, people are thinking about expanding horizons with new ideas and technologies. High risk shares perform better in this situation.

Another consideration to make when buying penny stocks is gross domestic product (GDP). GDP refers to the value of the good and services in the country. This will help you determine how the market is doing. If the GDP is high, it means that the economy is doing well.

You should also think about the yields and dividends of shares when you decide to buy. If the share price is high, it means that the yield is low. As an investor, you will get dividends for most of the shares you buy. Such shares are more stable in terms of offering dividend but the value does not increase as fast as growth shares.

As an investor, you should not be attached to particular shares. Some investors decide to stick to one share regardless of the reports and circumstances in the market, which may lead to huge losses.

THE RIGHT TIME TO BUY STOCKS

So when is the right time to buy stocks? When can a person buy a stock while being sure of making some good profits?

Timing is a very critical factor in the world of investment, buying the share you intended to buy few months later may result in either reducing your profits or maximizing your gains. Some stocks go up more than 10 percent in one day while some others drop with the same amount, buying a stock before or after that day can certainly affect your investment income, and that's why it's very important to try to pay attention to your timing.

What to buy, is more important than when to buy

Chartists or people who only depend on technical analysis to make investment decisions may buy a company that is on the edge of bankruptcy just because its chart looks good and they don't take into consideration the fact that, unless you buy a company not a stock, you won't be able to make money and you may face a catastrophic event.

Knowing what stock you are going to buy and knowing the exact reason you are buying it is crucial to making a great return on investment. For instance, knowing that you are buying a wine company's stocks because it has dominant market share, a strong competitive advantage and a satisfactory dividend is a great example of buying something that you know or that you understand.

Buying stocks of a company that you understand everything about is a key factor to making money out of the stock market, after all, industry trends, introduction of new products and competition are among the factors that affects share prices directly. If you did not have an understanding of the industry that your stock belongs to you're leaving much to chance and the possibility of losing money greatly increases.

The right time to buy stocks

Suppose that you decided to buy shares of a mining company that extracts gold, bearing in mind that gold prices affect the company's shares. If for example the price of gold went up, the company will make more profit and its shares will rise and vice versa. In such a case you should watch for declines in gold prices and see their effect on your stock's price. As soon as you realize that further declines in gold prices are no longer affecting the stock's price then this may be a perfect opportunity to buy it.

It's not necessary that the stock becomes tied to commodity like gold, after all stocks are subject to many other factors that can affect their own prices just like gold's prices affect mining companies. Interest rate changes, tax rates, input prices and inflation are among the factors that affects almost every traded stock.

If your stock prices go down when there's an increase in interest rates, then you should look for the time when further rate increases won't affect the price any more. At this point the stocks have reached a level where investors aren't willing to dump them at lower prices and the reason why buying at that point makes a lot sense. If interest rates went up further, the price won't move that much and if the opposite happened you will start to make money.

Of course stocks will always keep responding to the external variables and that's why it is advised to notice the degree to which they respond to these variables; as soon as the degree becomes lower, then it may be an indication that stock won't go down any further.

CHEAPEST WAY TO BUY STOCKS

Keep in mind that if you truly want to walk away with significantly more money than when you started, you need to pay attention to your costs. This might sound weird or even crazy. After all, you and most other investors have probably heard that when trading in the market, people should focus on picking the right stocks and getting in and out at just the right time. Everything else, according to this line of advice, is not as important.

A position in stock trading is the position you take when you buy or sell securities. When buying a stock, future or option, it is described as a "Long Position". In the other hand, when selling it is described as 'short position'.

If you follow conventional wisdom about trading fees, you would join the ranks of many traders who see a significant chunk of their earnings go to trading fees. Why? Depending on your investing style and how you play the market, your expenses might increase a lot as you take up positions. In fact, for momentum traders, trading fees can burn a hole through their bottom line since momentum traders' trade many times in any given day.

Similarly, day traders can get in and out of a position many times in the span of a week. If you don't pay attention to your trading fees, these fees might eat your profits. Think about it-you worked hard to rack up some solid returns and it can be a true waste of time and effort to see a large chunk of your hard-earned cash wasted in the form of fees.

Thanks to the rise of Internet-based trading, the average cost of stock trading has dropped tremendously. There are lots of discount online trading services on the market. There is a bidding war for your business and this is definitely a great thing for investors from a cost perspective. The downside with the cheaper options is, of course, that you usually don't get any advice or value-added services bundled in with these discount brokerage services. They tend to focus on making sure that your order to buy or sell stocks goes through quickly and accurately. The good news is that if you are in need of these cheap trading services, you probably already know what you'll be trading. You probably already know what you're doing. Make no mistake about it-low cost discount stock brokers aren't for amateur stock investors or people who need their hand held through the investment process. While discount brokers are the cheapest practical stock brokerage options out there, there are cheaper methods available. However, they might not necessarily apply to your situation.

What's the cheapest way to buy stocks?

The cheapest way to buy stocks is to buy it through your employer. There are many downsides to this. First of all, most people don't work for companies that sell their own company stock to employees in the form of payroll low cost stock buying deductions. Moreover, not all public companies have such programs.

Finally, such programs only offer the company's stock to the employees of the company. It is no surprise that only a very few people qualify for this way of buying stocks. Still, if you want to save money on broker fees, this is definitely, hands down, the cheapest way to buy stocks. If you are like most other members of the general public, your best bet in buying stocks the cheapest way possible is to use a discount broker.

How to pick the best discount broker for your needs

There are so many discount brokers being advertised on the Internet and on cable TV finance shows that it can be very confusing as to which service to go with. Don't be confused. Choosing the right broker actually is easier than you think. The first step to making the right choice is to understand that 'the best' doesn't really exist. What is 'best' for one person might be flat out wrong for another person.

Instead of focusing on 'the best,' focus on what's right for your particular situation and needs. Pick the right discount broker for your needs. Viewed from this perspective, many traders realize that the 'best' broker might not necessarily be the cheapest. There might be other factors like speed of execution or wide market coverage that makes them gravitate towards one particular broker over several others. To find out what makes the most sense in your particular trading situation, keep the following factors in mind.

Account minimums

The first thing to pay attention is the account minimum. The amount you have to invest will have a huge impact on the options you have available. Brokers have a minmum as a requirement mainly because it can be very hard for them to make money off very small accounts.

If you don't have much money to start with, don't worry. There are highly ranked brokers that do not have an account minimum. However, if you have specific requirements on your list that ask for a broker with a higher account minimum, it is worth it to save enough money and start when you have enough.

Ease of access

How easy is it to access the broker's trading platform? Most discount traders have an online platform and this might lead you to think 'once you've seen one online trading platform, you've seen them all.' You'd be keeping trading on the cheap side absolutely mistaken if you think this way. Sure, many online traders use online interfaces and they seem to use the same processes but that's where the similarities end. You need to look under the hood and see how fast, how secure, and how redundant their systems are. In short, how easily can you access and use these platforms? Not all platforms are reliable. Not all provide lightning quick executions.

Account fees

While it's hard to avoid account fees completely, you can definitivale minimize them. Several brokers charge a fee for doing certain transactions such as transferring funds or closing an account. A lot of fees can be avoided by choosing a broker that either doesn't charge them or by not selecting specific services they offer. Some of the most common fees you'll find are: Inactivity fees, broker assisted fees, periodic fees (such as annual fees) and trading platform fees.

Your trading style and tech needs.

When selecting a broker, it's important to tak in consideration your trading style and tech needs. For example, if you're a beginner investor, you're probably not going to be trading frequently. Because of this, it would be a good idea to avoid brokers that will charge you an inactivity fee. If you would like to use your mobile device for transactions, make sure that the broker has a great app that's intuitive, easy to use and works flawlessly on your device.

You might be looking for a little education or advice. In this case you should select a broker that includes tools for you to expand your learning.

Looking beyond the cheapest fees to buy stocks: Security and Speed

If you need a short summary of the two biggest factors that separate solid online brokers from their competitors, you need to look past the cheap fees. Sure, many online platforms can offer cheap fees, but what separates them is security and speed. Great online trading platforms offer top notch security and lightning fast executions. The latter is particularly crucial if you are doing momentum trading.

With momentum trading, you need to get in and out of stock positions with good timing so you can scoop up small movements in share prices that translate to a decent profit or a sizable loss. This is why speed is essential. You don't want to miss an opportunity or get caught in a position in a downtrend.

While looking for the cheapest online broker is important, you need to make sure you add a few more considerations to your search. Don't just go for the cheapest trading service. Make sure you also factor in security and speed of execution. These factors give you peace of mind as well as improve your chances of making more money in the fast-paced world of stock trading.

Direct Re-Investment Plans (DRIPS) and Direct Investment Plans (DIPS)

As we've learned, we may buy stocks through a broker, the most common way for buying stocks, where you are hiring broker who will manage and buy stocks for you in both markets or from companies which offer it directly. But there's also Direct Re-Investment Plans (DRIPS) and Direct Investment Plans (DIPS).

With these, you don't need a lot of money to start investing. It is possible to being with next to nothing because DRIPs give you the option of investing as little as $30 or $60 directly into your own account with the company, which sidesteps the need for a broker, making you avoid fees and commissions. This is a good option for starters since there is lesser risk involved as you did not spend much. When everything has been studied by you, which includes the reading of the stock flow in the market, then you might one day consider having a broker of your own when you have plans of accumulating more stocks.

Chapter 4: Buying stocks online through a broker

There's a few steps you'll need to before you get your hands on the stocks you're interested in. Make sure that you are careful and don't skip any of the following steps.

Let's start with buying stocks through a broker.

Register with a Discount Broker

By now you know how important it is to take some time to select the best option based on your needs. If possible, create a discount brokerage comparison chart so that you can compare and contrast all the things that you can get and the things that you need to pay for when you work with a broker. Make sure that you include trading, maintenance, as well as the different fees when you assess how much brokerage will burn a hole in your pocket for a long period of time. Once you have found the one that suits all your needs as well as your budget, it's time to sign up.

Add Funds to Your Account

Of course, you need to have money in your account so that you will be able to purchase the stocks. The boker you've selected should have an easy way for you to add funds. Some brokers give you the option of transferring funds from your bank account to the brokerage account. You may also want to explore post paid bill payment in case you want to have a more secure type of funding for your account. Once you have the right amount of funds, you are basically ready to start trading.

Shopping for stocks

It is important for you to "window shop" for stocks that you wish to purchase. Ask for quotes, read about the companies that you are interested in, and follow the ebb and flow of the stock market. Make sure that you are informed about the current quotes on the stocks that you are eyeing on. Try to look into the last price, bid, asking price, and the volume or number of shares that the stocks are traded for several days. Study the stocks that you want to purchase so you would know where to place your money and how to go with the whole process of trading fast and carefully.

Begin Trading

Once you have prepared your account, and feel confident enough in your knowledge about the current stocks on trade then you are ready to start trading. This is the time to examine the financial wellbeing of different companies and the rise and fall of their stocks over the past so that you narrow it down to only those that adhere to your requirements and goals as an investor. It's important to make the right decisions even at the very beginning so that you are sure that your money will grow and your investment is worth it.

THINGS YOU NEED TO KNOW ABOUT BUYING STOCKS ONLINE YOUR BROKER WON'T USUALLY TELL YOU

Here are things that are critically important about trading or investing online using a retail broker:

1. All brokers are required to adhere to specific rules and regulations. One of those rules that will affect you at some point is the Compliance Officer that is resident in the brokerage firm. This person is a "police officer" so to speak who makes sure that the broker is performing and acting in compliance to all the rules and regulations of the SEC and the US stock market or other markets. Compliance Officers are your best friend if you discover

that you have had a "bad fill" or an "out of the National Best Bid Offer" price.

If you find that your order was improperly filled or not executed per your order specifications, you must contact the Compliance Officer within 24 hours, the sooner the better and report your claim. You must also have a record aka a printed copy of your order, in order to prove what you entered and show why the order execution is not compliant with the regulations.

That means each time you enter an order be sure to print off a copy and keep it in your files. These out of NBBO orders are not common but when and if they occur, you need to know to take immediate action. If the order was filled improperly then the order will be reversed, and you will have your capital back and be out of the stock.

2. Online Brokers are a highly competitive oligopoly right now with only a few competing for the individual investor and trader revenues with their products and services. Therefore some are offering to give new customer money or other offers, but be wary of these brokers. Remember that they are in the business of making money from fees, charges for transactions, and order processing.

If they are paying you to sign up with them, consider how they are going to get all that money back AND make a profit. Most of the time they do this by charging higher fees or by slippage. Slippage is the difference between The Bid and The Ask. Normally this is very small, a few pennies nowadays but some brokers take advantage of slippage constantly and over time this can cost you a lot of money. There also may be hidden fees and charges. The broker is in business to make money, so giving you money makes no sense unless they can get that money back and then some quickly.

3. Broker competition has created an increasing complexity to online order processing. If you are not a Day trader then all you need is a simple order screen with bracketed order capability, where you can place a controlled order to keep you from getting filled on a gap or fast running stock.

In addition online broker charting software is inferior and inadequate for most individual investors and traders. Having all of your trading tools with one vendor is not a good idea. Having separate charting software that is complete is better. The reason is because a Charting Software company is doing one thing, which is designing the best charting software for specific trading styles. This means it will have the tools and resources that are not available in the basic, canned charting offered by brokers.

4. Never use an "At Market Order" except if you need to sell out of a stock quickly. Never use a simple "Limit Order." The reason is that online brokers are registered and licensed to sell you stocks or whatever instrument you are trading or investing in. Stock Broker means Stock Salesman. Always view your broker in the same way you would approach a car salesperson, a realtor, or any other professional sales person. They are selling stocks instead of something else.

As a sales company for stocks, they are permitted to buy stocks at a much lower price and then turn around and sell those stocks to you as the price goes up. "At Market" means that you are being filled at whatever price the stock is currently being offered at, which could be much higher than you expect if the stock is running and particularly in the early morning as the markets open and High Frequency Trading Firms automated trigger orders cause major gap ups.

Even worse than that are "Limit Orders" when brokers
make a huge amount of money as a stock is falling and
you buy into that stock. So now you are in a stock that is
moving down and could potentially fall a lot more.
These two types of orders make brokers a lot of profits.
These two types of orders cause most of the losses for
individual traders.

5. Day trading is a trading style that makes some brokers
a lot of money. However this is not the best nor the
most profitable trading style for individual traders. It is
not as easy as it sounds and in fact over the past decade
with the new decimal system for the bid/ask and High
Frequency Trading, day trading has become even more
difficult to learn and far more challenging to make
money. Online brokers encourage day trading because
they make a huge amount of money when individual
traders trade frequently.

The more orders entered the more profits the broker makes. Their "training courses" are not written by certified experts, but are targeted to keep you trading more often. A reputable day trading broker will require a significantly higher capital base because you will be using margin most of the time. The reputable broker will require that you pass an exam before they will allow you to day trade. The goal of trading should be for you to make good profits, and not give all your hard earned money to an online broker.

6. Full Service Broker versus Discount Brokers. Full service brokers offer advice and have staff to help you learn how to place an order in their online trading system. Discount brokers typically do not have staff on hand to assist you. You must figure out the online trading system and order processing on your own.

Full service costs are much higher as they have people there to help you and answer questions. Choose based on your experience level and requirements.

7. The goal of the online broker is to make their firm a huge amount of money from selling their products and services. It is not to help you be profitable or successful. Never think that they are your best friend because they are business people, and you must keep that perspective. They will not offer you something for free unless they are going to make a huge amount of money from you.

Make sure that your broker is a member and insured by the SPIC which is the brokerage account version of the FDIC. Ask around about other individual investor and trader experiences with different brokers. Most brokers have nearly identical products and services so what really matters is how well your orders are executed, the amount of slippage, the response to your questions or concerns, support, and compliance. Be sure and do your homework before ever signing up with any online broker.

Chapter 5: Buying stocks without a broker

Maybe you're interested in buying stocks yourself, without using a broker. To some, it may sound complicated or even scary. However the answer is probably a lot simpler then what you might expect. In reality, buying stocks through a broker is diminishing in popularity somewhat, but it used to be the only way to buy stocks.

Now that we have widespread internet access, we are able to bypass traditional brokers, and their sometimes sky high fees, and simply go straight to the source. So if you're a beginner investor and you want to buy stocks without a broker, it's actually very simple, and most likely the best way for you to go about investing in stocks, options, commodities etc... Let's take a closer look below at some of the specifics for buying stocks without a broker, as a beginner.

What Platform to Use as a Beginner

If you're a beginner, stay away from all the gimmicky Forex and stock trading platforms, and try to find a solid reliable online trading platform. Some of the best ones can be set up through your bank. Buying stock without a broker is a lot cheaper than the traditional way, but you will still be charged anywhere from $1 to $20 for a single trade.

If you're more advanced, you can find some online trading platforms that will allow you to buy stocks with live features, such as moving charts, with live bids/ask stats, and much more. Back to the beginner aspects of buying stocks without a broker, once you have your account set up, it's up to you to search for the stocks that you want to buy. Usually this is done by entering the company's ticker symbol, but can sometimes also be found by just entering the company name.

Buying the Stocks without a Broker

Once you have done all your stock research, and you have located your stock inside your online trading platform, you can then view the stats. Inside a very basic trading platform, like the one provided by your bank, you can usually view the stock chart in different views. The stock chart should show you the 5 year, 4 year, 3 year, 2 year, and 1 year history. Along with this information, you should also be able to view volume of the stocks and sometimes the bid/ask.

When you're ready to buy the stock, you can put in your bid. You can make this bid anything you want, so if you want to buy the stock lower than it is, you can put in a low bid, although it may never get filed. If you're confident enough and you want to buy the stock at the current price, just place a bid at the market value, your bid will then get "filled" and you will own the stocks. As simple as that!

You can also buy stocks without using a broker by enrolling in a Dividend Reinvestment Program (DRIP). DRIPS let you take cash dividends that are paid out by the organization you own a part of and use that money to buy more shares. The fees are usually minimal or even nonexisten depending on the specifics of each plan. You can quickly see the benefits, since a typical stock pays dividends around four times per year. Over a 10 year period, that's a lot of transactions on which you aren't paying any commissions. That being said, there are many brokers available that will reinvest dividend earnings at no extra cost for their clients, so if you find a broker that fits your requirements and has this option, these plans may not have much appeal.

DRIPs are often accompanied by cash investment options that are very similar to direct stock buying plans so that you can have periodic money withdrawals from your checking or savings account, or also have the option of sending one time payments whenever you'd like to buy more shares of stock.

Buying stocks online also gives you many important options that are also available with a regular broker, such as a stop, which will automatically sell your stocks if they sink to the low price you have placed your stop at, which is very important to avoid huge losses. It may take you a few weeks to get used to everything, but once used to it, you will wonder why anybody would ever pay 5 times the price for a broker. After making your first buy you usually have to wait 24hrs to see your new stock holdings in your online trading account.

Chapter 6: Buying stocks below market price

Maybe you've found a broker that has all the requirements you're looking for, but you aren't able to reach the account minimum. Or perhaps you're simply looking for ways to stretch your money and buy as many stocks as possible. Why would you ever pay full price when it's so easy to buy stocks at a discount?

Here's a few tips that may help you find great deals:

Enter a limit order to buy stocks:

A limit order lets you specify the price you want to pay, so just enter a lower price than the current market price and catch the stock on a dip. Of course, if the stock doesn't dip, there's no way to get the lower price.

Buy stocks at a limit price between the buy and ask price:

If you enter a market order to buy stock, you pay what's called the "Ask" price. If you enter a market order to sell stock, you will receive the "Bid" price. As you might expect, the Ask price is higher than the Bid price. So to get a small discount, just enter a limit order between the Bid and the Ask price. For many stocks, you will actually save enough to cover your commissions using this technique. Some of the more popular stocks have a Bid-Ask spread of only one penny; obviously, in those cases, this technique won't work.

Buy your stocks through a DRIP offering discount dividend re-investments:

Not all... but many..., DRIP stocks also offer a discount when you purchase shares through the company's DRIP plan. The discount typically ranges between 2% and 5%.

If the stock you want to buy offers a discount DRIP, buy at least one share "in your name"... which means you will take ownership of an actual stock certificate rather than letting your broker hold it. Then sign up for the DRIP directly with the company. Afterwards, every time a dividend is paid, you will buy shares up to 5% below the market price at that time.

Buy shares outright from the company:

Many stocks that offer a DRIP also offer shareholders the privilege to buy more shares directly from the company. When you do this, you often will pay no commission since there is no broker involved. However, many of these companies also offer a discount price when you buy directly from the company. The discount typically ranges from 3% to 5%. To do this, join the DRIP as described above. Then contact the company, and tell them how many shares you want to buy and get one to thousands of shares up to 5% below the market price at that time.

Chapter 7: When to sell stocks

Knowing when's the right time to buy stock is just as important as knowing when to buy them. This is a critically important skill for the savvy investor, after all most people buy and sell largely based on emotions. When it comes to selling, people often unload their stocks in a panic because of fears the market will collapse and they'll lose all their money. But, a savvy investor doesn't let fear guide his actions, and prefers to rely on planning instead. There are times when selling is a good move, but a bit of planning ahead should be always be included when investing in stocks. Here is some time tested advice to guide you:

1. Selling when your financial goals have been realized

By now you know that each time you make an investment, you should be planning out ahead of time what you want that investment to do for you. The goal of investing is to make money, not to keep stocks you hit the grave. The savvy investor sets concrete financial goals that include time deadlines and what they expect the investment to do for them. Example-you buy $5,000 of XYZ stock with the goal of doubling your money in 5 years.

When the 5 years are up, it's time to look at your investment and see how it's done. If your goal has been met, selling might be an option. If your goal hasn't been met, it may be time for a reassessment. For instance, if you're sitting at $9,000 when you hoped the stock would go up to $10,000, it might be time to unload your shares anyway (at least you made a profit), or you might decide to wait out another six months to see if you get where you wanted to go.

2. Things aren't working out

Deciding when to sell stock often boils down to a failed investment. If a stock isn't giving you good returns, why keep it? Of course it's important to give a company a reasonable amount of time to observe results. One year isn't enough time, but three to five years shoud be more than enough time to evaluate your investments. If your investment in XYZ stagnates or drops over the 5 year period, it may be time to sell.

3. You've found a better place for your money

After 3 years, XYZ is up to $6,000, but you've been eying ABC Company, whose stock has been rising rapidly and they have a favorable PEG ratio. It might be a good idea to sell your stock at this point in XYZ and reinvest the money in ABC.

4. Fundamentals going down

Knowing when to sell stock can often boil down to an evaluation of company fundamentals. If a company is not healthy, selling shares and reinvesting in something else is a good idea. However, be sure to give the company a reasonable time period to turn things around. Generally, this can be a 3-5 years time period. If a company is not showing signs of returning to profitability after 3 years, then it could be time to look elsewhere.

5. Stock market crash

On historical occasions, such as the tech bubble burst, the great recession of 2008 or the great depression, it might be time to bail on stocks completely. Many investors move to bonds and cash (or even gold) during tough economic times. This may be an option for selling your holdings. However, proceed with care. Moves of this type are often based on panic-and history has shown that waiting can prove rewarding.

Deciding how to "time the markets" will depend on your overall investment situation. If you're 25, you may be able to ride out a great economic crisis because in 15 years when things will have recovered you'll only be 40. But if you're 60, you'll want to move assets into more protected securities like bonds because you simply don't have time to wait around. Just make sure that whatever you do your market moves are based on sound financial planning and not hysterical panic.

Recognizing stock trends

One of the key elements to succeed as a trader is your ability to recognize stock trends. When you are able to recognize the major trends in stock market trading, you will better know when to sell stocks.

Here are some general ideas to identify the major trends in stock market:

1. Bull market & Bear market

Most of stocks, if not all, move with the market. It can be in a bull market or in a bear market.

Bull: In a bull market most stocks will steadily grow and indicates the presence of more buyers than sellers. Those who buy stock in a bull market are considered bullish traders

Bear: In a bear market most stocks will steadily slowly lose value and indicates the presence of more sellers than buyer. Those who sell stock in a bear market are considered bearish traders.

2. Price

To determine a trend you need to have information of the stock market price. The price tells you about the direction of movement of stocks and is determined by knowledge, hopes, fears, and expectations of all those people who already own the stock or might be thinking of owning it.

3. Volume

To determine a trend you also need to have information of the stock market volume. The volume tells you the amount of stocks being traded and whether there is movement in the stock market.

4. Trends

When you put price and volume together you will see whether there are more sellers or buyers in the stock market.

Up trend: In cases when you have both high volume and high price, these indicate an uptrend in stock market. Based on this, you may decide to buy the stock.

Downward trend: In cases when you have high volume but low price, these indicate a downward trend in stock market. Based on this, you may decide to sell the stock.

False signal: Quite often, when a stock move up or down it seems for you like a change in the trend. However, if you look further at the volume you may see that there is not enough volume for a stock to move up or down. In these cases, you should not expect a trend change in stock market, but a false signal.

Selling stocks without a broker

While selling stocks with a broker can be as simple as doing a couple of clicks, selling without one involves more steps. You may seek to bypass the intermediaries because of the fees rendered which reduce the profit margins of the transactions by increasing cost.

Here are five ways that could help you sell stocks without using the services of a broker.

Direct transfer to a third party

After finding and agreeing with an interested party, you can change the name of the shareholder to a different name of the new owner. Transferring stock to a third party is basically changing the ownership and the right to manage the stock. The entire process of changing ownership of stock can be facilitated by the company's investor relations office which most likely has contracted a transfer agent to handle the entire process on behalf of the firm.

Direct purchase plans

Many blue chip companies have provisions for investor relations whereby investors can directly buy or sell the particular company's stocks. Some companies charge a competitive fee for using their in-house services while others offer these services free of charge. Selling stocks directly offer the stock owner unadulterated per share pricing that is higher than the per share price proposed by brokers because of the reduced amount and types of fees in the entire process.

Dividend reinvestment plans

Company operated dividend reinvestment plans (DRIPs) are arrangements made by stockholders to reinvest the dividends earned from the investment without going through a brokerage facility. Putting this profit back in the company enables the shareholder to increase their stake in the company at a determined price per share without being charged commissions. However, the stockholder may only sell these shares back to the company or other shareholders with DRIP when offloading this stock and hence the intermediary is bypassed.

Become a broker

Another way of avoiding the dealers is to become an agent yourself. By acquiring brokerage accounts, one can sell stock on your behalf and behalf of other stockholders directly to the company. However, this process might be expensive for individual investors with small volumes because opening a brokerage account requires an initial deposit whose value is determined by the market regulators.

Selling directly to the company

Listed companies have investor relations departments that may allow share certificate holders to walk in and submit the stock certificate at the prevailing market price per share and the company deposits the equivalent in cash to the seller's preferred mode of payment. Consequently, this process can be facilitated by the transfer agent of the company who is contracted independently as an outsourced service provider and not as a broker.

Chapter 8: Mistakes to avoid and golden nuggets of advice

Trading can be challenging, but most of all it is risky. Successful investors and traders all agree that making mistakes is an unavoidable part of the learning process. However, you do not have to repeat the mistakes done by others. We can all learn something from the mistakes they've done.

Here are four of the most common mistakes that you should avoid in the stock market for a successful career in trading.

Using margin

As a new investor, you should never be lured by what is presented as free money. A margin is money extended to you by your broker as credit. Without experience in trading, buying on margin could land you in unnecessary debt. Stick to buying stock using your capital which places you within the risk profile that your capital allows you. This way, even if your positions do not yield, you get to live to trade another day. When your investments all flop and you bought them using margin, you land into debt in addition to losing your capital.

Chasing stocks

Wise investment entails purchasing a stock at the right share prices and selling when the price hits your desirable point or when the loss cannot be sustainable. Chasing the sock entails trying to fill an order by bidding successively as the rice moves. This is reactionary bidding, and you might lose your focus pursuing an order without being strategic about the risks and leverage that you hold. Avoid this at all costs. Purchase at the right time and pull out at the strategic time. Don't chase.

Don't hope

Trading is all about speculation, but don't be deceived that it is a game of hoping and praying for the stocks to turn in your favor. So don't hope. Instead, strategize based on philosophical and logical analysis of the market conditions. This is the only way that you will remain objective in selecting your positions and making the calls.

Buying stock hoping to sell them at a profit requires more than hope.

It requires discipline in sticking to your strategy and conducting performance analysis to determine how each trade performed, the lessons learned and your profits and losses.

This can be done by always carrying out a post-trade analysis.

Underestimating yourself

Most investors, especially beginners, have been scared to the point that they think less of themselves when it comes to excelling in the market. Success has somehow been reserved for the sophisticated investors with years of experience. But don't be deceived. Beginners can also be successful; it does not have to come after years of trading. However, it also depends on how you define success.

For a beginner, success should entail mastering a strategy that flips your $100 to $150 after two days. It is all about getting returns on your capital. And as you get used to trading, your capital also increases in line with your risk tolerance. That is the definition of success. So do not underestimate your abilities and potential to be a successful investor.

GOLDEN NUGGETS OF ADVICE

Before buying stocks, take a look at the 10 golden rules below. These rules should be the foundation of a healthy investment strategy.

1) Set a goal!

Set a target for your stock investments. Have realistic expectations. Shares are a long-term savings option, which historically has provided attractive returns.

2) Think long term!

Stock prices fluctuate up and down, but have always risen to new heights. Shares are accordingly not suited to short-term investments.

3) Invest regularly!

Never invest a big part of your savings in equities at a time. You might buy, while the shares are most expensive. Dividends should be reinvested and do not jump in and out of the stock market - it costs you just a lot of trading costs.

4) Spread Your Shopping!

Do not risk everything at once or on a few shares, but spread your investments in several companies, and preferably in different industries. Then you are less vulnerable to fluctuations in the individual company and industry. There's a reason why the 'don't put your eggs in one basket' is common advice said by stock investors. Diversification is a key element of any solid portfolio. At the same time, it's easy to overdo diversification. Research has found that the sweet spot seems to be a portfolio of 20 stocks. Any additional stocks from that point will only reduce risk minimally to the point which there is no more benefit to be gained.

Aso, it's not a matter of simply buying any 20 different stocks to be diversified. You should keep in mind that a properly diversified portfolio includes stocks that are different from each other. This could be based on factors such as organization size, industry, sector, location, etc. In other terms, you should be buying stocks that aren't too related to each other, so that they move in diferent directions and are affected by different factors.

5) Do your homework!

This is so important, it bears repeating: buy only shares in companies in which you are knowledgeable in. Buy shares in companies which for years have shown improvement in revenues and earnings - and stay informed about your shares.

6) Invest in open and shareholder-friendly companies!

Invest in companies that have an open and honest information policy and seek proper corporate governance (corporate governance).

7) Be wary of loans to equity investments!

It requires great care and experience in the stock market to buy shares with borrowed money. If it does not go as expected, the situation can be very difficult to handle.

8) Decide when you want to sell!

Keep your investments tidy and decide before purchase, when to sell - for example if a stock has fallen by 15%, or if one share has come to represent too large a share of your total portfolio.

9) Remember taxes!

There's no way around it, stocks are taxed. Whenever you sell stock, you'll have to pay taxes on the profits (but not on the entire sale amount). To calculate this, you simply need to substract what you paid for the stock originally from hor much you sold it for. Whenever you earn a positive capital gain, you'll be taxed on that number. Also, if your stock pays a dividend, the payout will be taxed.

10) Do not follow advice blindly!

Listen to others' advice, but follow them blindly. Be aware of your possible motives advisers to recommend one or the other. Banks should be seen and considered as sellers - not an impartial advisors.

Conclusion

Stocks are just one of the many possible options that investors have to make their hard earned money work for them. They have earned their popularity thanks to their high potential returns. Over the long term, you'll be hard pressed to find another type of investment that will perform better, especially for the average investor.

Now that you've finished reading this book, please make it a priority to continue learning and expanding your financial education. Start researching and analysing the performance of the companies and industries that you're interested in. Remember that you're more likely to make better decisions, get a better ROI and avoid damaging mistakes when you do your homework properly.

A next great step would be to learn about other types of investments you are interested in. A well diversified portfolio doesn't stop simply having stocks from several unrelated industries, locations, etc. An appropriate mix of investment options that are based on your individual requirements such as time, financial goals, and tolerance for risk. Whether you're interested in bonds or real estate, never forget to be always increasing your knowledge in this area.

Thank you, and good luck!

CPSIA information can be obtained
at www.ICGtesting.com
Printed in the USA
LVHW050032100221
678896LV00007B/734